# The Best websites for HOMEWORK

Recommended Websites for Key Stage 2

Andy Seed

Published in Great Britain in 2006 by Hodder Children's Books

Editor: Vic Parker
Design by Fiona Webb
Cover design by Hodder Children's Books



2



A Catalogue record for this book is available from the British Library

ISBN-10: 0 340 93037 3
ISBN-13: 978 0 340 93037 3

Printed and bound in Great Britain by Bookmarque Ltd, Croydon, Surrey

The paper and board used in this paperback by Hodder Children's Books are natural recyclable products made from wood grown in sustainable forests. The manufacturing processes conform to the environmental regulations of the country of origin.

Hodder Children's Books
a division of Hachette Children's Books
338 Euston Road
London NW1 3BH

# Contents

# introduction



The web can be a great place to find out things but, let's face it, it's full of rubbish too. In fact, there's so much junk out there that you can waste hours – and that's no good at all if you've got homework to do. That's where this book comes in: it contains only good, helpful websites that have been carefully chosen by jolly teacher-types to help you do your homework really well.

How do you use it? Just follow these tips to find the homework help you want and get the most out of the book:

- This book is divided into subjects and each subject is divided into the different topics you do at school. So first, check the Contents pages at the front for the subject you want. Then turn to the subject pages and find the topic you need. For instance, if you want help with fractions, first find *maths* in the Contents, then look in the *maths* section for the pages on *number*. However, you can also find help with fractions in many of the general maths sites listed too. This is true for most other subjects besides maths.

- If the web address given for a site is very long, try to type it very carefully. It may be easier to search for the home page of the website then follow links to the page you want. For example, the address for the Tracy Beaker *Pass the Story* site is

  **www.bbc.co.uk/cbbc/tracybeaker/tracysclub/passthestory/**

  If you just type *bbc* into your browser you'll get to the www.bbc.co.uk home page. From there you can click *CBBC*, then *Tracy Beaker*, then *Pass the Story*.

- All of the websites are free, but with some you may need to register or pay to see the full content. Ask at home if you think you need to do this for a particular site.

- Some of the websites listed have games and activities which require free software (called plugins), such as Flash, to play. Your computer probably has these already, but if not, you can download them easily from many of the websites which have games.

- Some games and activities help you to understand a topic better, so even if you're just looking for facts and information, it may be worth having a go at a game or interactive quiz.

# ENGLISH

# Spelling and vocabulary



## Spellits

Three fun Flash games from the BBC, with cartoons and plenty of noise. You have to solve a mystery in each game by completing spelling challenges – good fun to play with a friend.

**www.bbc.co.uk/schools/spellits/**

## Spelling Quizzes for Lower Juniors

A fantastic collection of quizzes and word activities which will help you to spell Y3 and Y4 words from the National Literacy Spelling Bank. All answers are marked for you too!

**www.saintambrosebarlow.wigan.sch.uk/lowerjuniorspelling.htm**

## Spelling Activities for Upper Juniors

Another great set of pages from the wonderful St Ambrose Barlow Primary School. Click on *Activities for Upper Juniors* or *Upper Junior Spellings* to find interactive quizzes, puzzles and more for Y5 and Y6.

**www.saintambrosebarlow.wigan.sch.uk/pupillinks.htm**

## Look-Cover-Write-Check

Here's a fun version of the good old spelling activity which helps you to learn those key words. Plenty of sound and action too.

**http://atschool.eduweb.co.uk/toftwood/lcwc.html**

## Word Level Games

This excellent page has links to over 20 games, chosen by nice primary school teachers, which will sharpen up your spelling and vocabulary. Try them.

**www.woodlands-junior.kent.sch.uk/interactive/literacy2.htm**

## Word Central

A way-cool American site which includes a *Daily Buzzword* to perk up your vocabulary. There are also activities and a chance to make your own nutty dictionary with invented words.

**www.wordcentral.com**

# Grammar



## Grammar Gorillas

A simple ape-based introduction to nouns, verbs, adjectives and the rest, with a help section and a multiple choice activity thrown in. You get a score at the end of the game.

**http://www.funbrain.com/grammar/index.html**

## BBC ReviseWise Grammar

Try the two grammar activities on this page – each one has animations, lots of examples and a test to do at the end. One is about complex sentences and the other covers adjectives and adverbs.

**www.bbc.co.uk/schools/revisewise/english/spelling**

## Star Punc

Some simple but useful online activities to pep up your punctuation: you have to put the missing punctuation marks into a set of stories by clicking.

**www.mape.org.uk/startower/starpunc/index.htm**

## Homework High: Punctuation

This ace site is aimed at KS3 kids but it's a big help if you have trouble with punctuation. There are 222 tips written by teachers! Click on *English* then *Punctuation* and browse through the questions.

**www.channel4.com/learning/microsites/H/homeworkhigh/index.html**

## Plural Nouns

Bags of useful info about how to make nouns into plurals, e.g. half → halves, tooth → teeth.

**http://www2.gsu.edu/%7Ewwwesl/egw/crump.htm**

## English Games

Tense about tenses? Forgotten what apostrophes are for? Look at this page of mixed activities which includes exercises to help sort you out.

**www.saintambrosebarlow.wigan.sch.uk/funandgames.htm**

# Reading: Fiction



## Book Box

Fab site from Channel 4 Learning: see and hear from over 30 top authors, poets and illustrators including Jacqueline Wilson and Anthony Horowitz; watch videos, play games, read book extracts and do loads more.

**www.channel4.com/learning/microsites/B/bookbox/home.htm**

## Solve the Mystery

Fancy being a detective? Reckon you can crack the case of the missing diamond necklace? For this activity and test you must find clues to solve a mystery by reading very carefully.

**www.bbc.co.uk/schools/revisewise/english/reading/02_act.shtml**

## Ozzie Takes a Ride

This fun interactive story about two rather brainy animals is aimed at Y3 and Y4 and is full of useful learning tips for reading.

**www.nwlg.org/pages/resources/owl/OWL3Book1/Book01/default.htm**

## The Official Roald Dahl Site

Cracking website all about the legendary children's author, with information, book extracts, a biography, pictures, games and more. Very noisy and entertaining.

**www.roalddahl.com**

## Myths and Legends

A simple site which features myths, legends and traditional stories from different times and places.

**http://home.freeuk.net/elloughton13/theatre.htm**

## Narnia Online

This glossy site has clips from the Narnia films as well as information about the books by CS Lewis.

**www.narnia.com**

# Reading: Fiction



**Mrs Mad**

Book reviews from Mrs Mad! You can search by title, author or age group.

**www.mrsmad.com**

**Readit**

Another very worthwhile book review site. You can search reviews by author, age group, type of book, title or number of stars. Send in your own reviews if you like: why not?

**www.readit.org.uk**

**Cool-Reads**

Book review site created and written by 10-to-15-year-olds. Very impressive it is too: every review is split into short sections and there's a star rating plus a picture of the book.

**www.cool-reads.co.uk**

**Author Profiles**

This page has links to the websites of many of today's popular children's authors, plus a page for each which tells you something about them.

**http://wordpool.co.uk/ap/apcontents.htm**

**Authors and Illustrators**

Links to the websites of hundreds of children's authors and illustrators. Great if you want to find out more about a particular writer or artist.

**http://ukchildrensbooks.co.uk/**

**Puffin.co.uk**

The Puffin books website has author info, facts about how books are made, extracts from books, games and plenty more fun stuff about reading.

**www.puffin.co.uk**

# Reading: Poetry



## Poetry Zone

Poetry book reviews, interviews with poets, writing tips, competitions and – not surprisingly – poems. You can send in your own work too.

**www.poetryzone.ndirect.co.uk/index2.htm**

## ReviseWise Poetry

A neat Flash activity looking at a challenging poem, plus a test and worksheet you can print out too. You get some helpful feedback with the test.

**www.bbc.co.uk/schools/revisewise/english/reading/**

## Fridge Poetry

Have a go at making up your own poems by dragging words from ready-made lists. Fun and very creative!

**www.bbc.co.uk/arts/poetry/wordplay/game.shtml**

# Reading: non-Fiction

### An Introduction to Non-Fiction Books

A simple slide show which tells you about the features of non-fiction books. There are no pictures so it's a good idea to have an information book with you while you look at the site.

**www.primaryresources.co.uk/english/powerpoints/non-fiction_books.swf**

### ReviseWise Non-Fiction

Let ace cartoon librarian, Henrietta Hush, help you to learn a few nifty things about non-fiction books. There is also an interactive test and a worksheet to download if you're keen.

**www.bbc.co.uk/schools/revisewise/english/reading/**

### Write a News Report

Find out what's involved in putting together a newspaper report.

**www.ngflcymru.org.uk/vtc/20041115/English/Keystage2/Writing/Bignews**

# Writing: General Sites



## Writing With Writers

A brilliant site where you are given guidance by authors to write stories, poetry, and non-fiction including reviews, reports and biographies.

**http://teacher.scholastic.com/writewit/index.htm**

## Stories From the Web

An excellent site where you can send in your own stories, poems and reviews, as well as learn about authors and how they write. There are activities and competitions too.

**www.storiesfromtheweb.org**

## Discover Writing

A treasure-trove of ideas, tips, examples, rules, advice, quotes, extracts and more from this American site.

**www.discover-writing.com/forstudents.html**

## Better Writing

Tip top tips on spelling, grammar, writing letters, using plain English and lots more from the clever Oxford English Dictionary people.

**www.askoxford.com/betterwriting/?view=uk**

## Kids on the Net

A place where you can get your poetry and other writing published online – if it's good! The site also has pages of hints and an introduction to digital writing.

**http://kotn.ntu.ac.uk**

## Telling Tales

Here's a good assortment of things to do with writing. Try out some of the activities such as *Story Starters* or *Characters* – they will hopefully give you ideas for writing.

**www.tellingtales.com/Stufftodo/StuffToDo.htm**

# Writing: Fiction



## Planning a Story

Here's an animated activity to help you learn about characters, settings, plot and timescale. As usual with BBC ReviseWise, there's an online test to check up on what you know too.

**www.bbc.co.uk/schools/revisewise/english/writing/**

## Story Writing

Straight advice from the superb Woodlands Junior School in Kent – includes sections on writing better sentences and using direct speech.

**www.woodlands-junior.kent.sch.uk/English/story.html**

## Pass the Story

Reckon you can write a paragraph of a story started by Jacqueline Wilson? Here's your chance.

**www.bbc.co.uk/cbbc/tracybeaker/tracysclub/passthestory/**

## Write a Monster Poem

A clever little page with an interactive writing frame, plus pop-up boxes of words and advice, to help you create a winning monster poem.

**www.lancsngfl.ac.uk/curriculum/literacy/lit_site/html/fiction/my_monster/index.htm**

## Using Similes

Bring your poetry writing alive by using similes. Click *Teaching Resources* then *Key Stage* 2 then *English* then *Writing* then *Style* then *Using Similes* … Phew!

**www.ngfl-cymru.org.uk/index-new.htm**

## Rhyming Dictionary

Just type in the word you want to find a rhyme for and see what comes up. Fantastic!

**www.rhymezone.com/**

# Writing: Non-Fiction

## Writing Non-Fiction

Top help from the BBC with writing instructions, letters and leaflets.

**www.bbc.co.uk/schools/revisewise/english/writing/**

## Writing a Book Review

Advice from Factmonster about writing a good book review (they call it a book report but we'll forgive them). Look out for the canny *Word Wise* section on this site too.

**www.factmonster.com/homework/wsbookreportelem.html**

## Recounts

Here are some really interesting examples of recounts about people's experiences during World War II. You need to click on *Non-Fiction* and then *World War II Recounts*.

**www.lancsngfl.ac.uk/curriculum/literacyresources/index.php**

# maths

# General Sites



## ReviseWise Maths

15 activities with interactive tests from the BBC covering all of the main areas of maths which you need to know at KS2. Just the job for SATs revision.

**www.bbc.co.uk/schools/revisewise/maths**

## Maths Booster

This is a great place to check up on what you know and get practising what you don't know using some cool Flash games.

**www.bgfl.org/mathsbooster**

## Count On

Oodles of brilliant games, activities, ideas, pictures, facts and even poems connected with numbers and maths. One to explore!

**www.counton.org/**

## Maths is Fun

You might not believe it … but it can be! Click the menu on the left to see how it explains different topics such as percentages or angles.

**www.mathsisfun.com**

## Woodlands Maths Page

Here is a smart page of links taking you to activities and websites covering the different areas of KS2 maths. Very useful.

**www.woodlands-junior.kent.sch.uk/maths/index.html**

## The Math Page

Yes, it's American but ignore the missing 's' on 'math' and give it a go: it has lots of good explanations of how to do things.

**www.themathpage.com**

# numbers



## Maths in the Factory

This is all about chocolate! Sharpen up your number skills with Cadbury's – click on *Learning Zone* then *Maths in Chocolate Making* for five sets of useful activities.

**www.cadburylearningzone.co.uk/maths/**

## Number Games

A big range of online games to help your brain become sharper with numbers. The activities are mainly about adding and subtracting.

**www.woodlands-junior.kent.sch.uk/maths/numberskills.html**

## Digger and the Gang

Cool animated adventures with number puzzles to solve along the way.

**www.bbc.co.uk/schools/digger**

## Fractions

A set of animated online activities to help you understand all about quarters and tenths.

**www.bgfl.org/bgfl/custom/resources_ftp/client_ftp/ks2/maths/fractions/index.htm**

## Fractotron

Fun fractions game made by pupils at Ambleside Primary School.

**www.amblesideprimary.com/ambleweb/mentalmaths/fractotron.html**

## Decimals

This Canadian site is magic for learning about decimals. Click *Grade 6* then *Mathematics* then *Spy Guys*. When the page loads click *Lessons* then *Decimals*.

**www.learnalberta.ca/Main.aspx**

# Calculations



## Times Tables

This page has loads of different types of activities and games to help you practise your multiplication tables. Get learning!

**www.woodlands-junior.kent.sch.uk/maths/timestable/index.html**

## Multiplication.com

Here you'll find a whole series of online lessons which explain multiplication to help you learn your tables. Can't be bad.

**www.multiplication.com/students.htm**

## Basket Maths

You can get plenty of practice at answering all sorts of maths questions here – and if you get them right, an animated basketball player scores a basket.

**www.scienceacademy.com/BI**

## Sum Sense: Multiplication

A good way to practise your multiplying skills – see if you can beat the clock!

**www.oswego.org/ocsd-web/games/SumSense/summulti.html**

## Sum Sense: Division

Try these tough challenges to sharpen up your dividing. Well presented and enjoyable.

**www.oswego.org/ocsd-web/games/SumSense/sumdiv.html**

## Mental Maths

Swot up on addition, subtraction and lots of other things you need to do in your head, with the help of Woodlands Junior School.

**www.woodlands-junior.kent.sch.uk/maths/wordproblems/index.html**

# Solving Problems

## Nrich

All sorts of tricky maths puzzles at all sorts of levels, with hints and explanations of the solutions.

**www.nrich.maths.org**

## Puzzle Maths

Seven cool and challenging Flash games for you to try from Channel 4 Learning. Most of them involve number calculations.

**www.channel4.com/learning/microsites/P/puzzlemaths/**

## Y6 Challenge

Some tough but fun games and puzzles designed to sharpen up your mental maths skills. Aimed at Year 6.

**www.echalk.co.uk/Maths/PrimaryNationalStrategy_Yr6/DfES-MathsActivitiesforyear6/index.html**

### Word Problems

Do you get stuck with those long written questions in maths? I do too! This page offers you help, with some good examples to follow.

**www.icteachers.co.uk/children/sats/maths_problems.htm**

### Mental Machine

Try this set of mental maths problems from Ambleside Primary School. You can then try to beat your last score.

**www.amblesideprimary.com/ambleweb/mentalmaths/mentalmachine2.html**

### Maths Mysteries

Help two detectives by solving puzzles in this fun interactive challenge.

**www.counton.org/mathsmysteries/**

# Measures, Shape and Space



## Measuring to the Nearest Half cm or mm

An easy-to-follow presentation to help you measure shapes using cm and mm – just click the screen to see each slide.

**www.primaryresources.co.uk/maths/powerpoint/measuring_nearesthalfcm_mm.swf**

## Shapes

Here's a cool way to learn about the properties of 2-D and 3-D shapes. It includes nets of shapes to print out so you can make your own.

**www.bgfl.org/bgfl/custom/resources_ftp/client_ftp/ks2/maths/3d/index.htm**

## Sorting Triangles

Do you know your scalenes from your isosceles? If not, you can gen up on triangles with this Flash activity.

**www.crick.northants.sch.uk/Flash%20Studio/cfsmaths/Triangles/triangles.swf**

### Symmetry

Try this game which helps you learn about lines of symmetry and shapes.

**www.innovationslearning.co.uk/subjects/maths/activities/year3/symmetry/shape_game.asp**

### Co-ordinates

Do you have trouble using co-ordinates to mark the position of a point? Try this simple practice activity.

**www.primaryresources.co.uk/online/coordinates.swf**

### Angle Activities

This is a great interactive page where you can measure angles using a protractor on screen. Recommended.

**www.amblesideprimary.com/ambleweb/mentalmaths/angleshapes.html**

# Handling Data



## M-G6

Awesome Canadian site for learning about probability and other tricky topics in maths. Click *Grade 6* then *Mathematics* then *Spy Guys*, then *Lessons*, then *Probability*.

**www.learnalberta.ca/Main.aspx**

## Interpreting Data

Learn about charts and graphs with this jolly Flash animation and test. There's even a worksheet to download if you're really keen.

**www.bbc.co.uk/schools/revisewise/maths/data/11_act.shtml**

## How to Find the Mean

A simple page about averages, with links to more help with data-handling topics such as median and mode.

**www.mathsisfun.com/mean.html**

### Chocolate Graphs

Learn about graphs and data with Cadbury's. Click *Maths in Chocolate Making*, then activity five: *Sort the Facts*.

**www.cadburylearningzone.co.uk/maths/index_content.htm**

### Create a Graph

Learn how different types of graph work by making one online using this clever website. Print out your results for top-quality presentation of data.

**http://nces.ed.gov/nceskids/createagraph/**

### Venn Diagram

This is a dinky drag-and-drop online activity which will help you to understand how Venn diagrams work.

**http://www.primaryresources.co.uk/online/venn.swf**

# Handling Data



## Data handling introductions

Here are four good clear pages introducing mean, median, mode and probability. There are no activities but it's a good place to go if you just want these topics explained to you.

**www.mathsisfun.com/data.html**

## Probability

Scroll down and you'll find links to three pages of help with the tricky subject of probability. There are lots of other useful maths revision links here too.

**www.icteachers.co.uk/children/children_sats.htm**

# Science

# General Sites



## Science Clips

Don't miss this ace collection of animations which help you learn about different aspects of science. Fun, clever and interesting.

**www.bbc.co.uk/schools/scienceclips/index_flash.shtml**

## Science Essentials

This site is split into three sections covering the natural world, materials and physical properties. Each section has basic info, answers to questions, a quiz and a glossary. No games, but still useful.

**www.channel4.com/apps26/learning/microsites/E/essentials/science/index.shtml**

## SOS Teacher

This page has links to over 100 questions asked by KS2 children about science and answered by teachers. Very useful for homework.

**www.bbc.co.uk/schools/revisewise/sosteacher/science/browse.shtml**

**Interactive Science**

Click on the topic you want to learn about, read the pages, then have a go at the activities to see if you know your onions!

**www.crick.northants.sch.uk/Flash%20Studio/cfsscience/cfsscience.htm**

**ReviseWise Science**

Go here for top-quality science activities, factsheets, tests and worksheets from the BBC – especially helpful if you have SATs coming up.

**www.bbc.co.uk/schools/revisewise/science**

**Science Revision**

Links to lots of different pages with activities, information, games, diagrams, pictures, animations and more, to help you become a science genius.

**www.woodlands-junior.kent.sch.uk/revision/Science/index.html**

# Life Processes and Living Things

## Biology: Life Processes and Living Things

Here you'll find facts on animals and plants, discover how they're grouped, learn what they do to stay alive, and a whole lot more – bingo!

**www.zephyrus.co.uk/biologykeystage2.html**

## My Body

You'll love this funky site with animations, jolly noises and lots of top-quality information about the body, health and growing up. It's well designed, helpful and not to be missed!

**www.kidshealth.org/kid/body/mybody.html**

## Bones

A simple introduction to the skeleton with facts about bones and what they're for, plus a neat little Flash game.

**www.bbc.co.uk/schools/podsmission/bones/**

**Food Fitness**

Information and advice about healthy eating and living a healthy lifestyle. There is a very useful set of pages on nutrition labels.

**www.foodfitness.org.uk/**

**Healthy Kids**

Click on your age at the bottom of the home page then find out what you want to know – there are sections on diet, drugs, illnesses, teeth, puberty, hygiene, and tons more.

**http://www.healthykids.org.uk/**

**Human and Animal Habitats**

Learn what sort of creatures live in the desert, the Antarctic, grasslands, forests and the sea – and why. The site has some very good multiple choice activities to do online.

**www.activescience-gsk.com/games/index.cfm?module=2**

### Planet Arkive

Tons of information about animals and plants, habitats, survival and endangered species. You'll also find excellent animations, videos, games, quizzes and activities.

**www.planetarkive.org**

### Nature Explorers

Explore the world of ponds, rivers, woodlands and grasslands online with this clear, helpful site. Have a go at the activities or try a web topic trail.

**www.naturegrid.org.uk/children.html**

### Living Rainforest

Get to know about poison frogs, giant millipedes, dwarf crocodiles and bananas. There are activity sheets to download too.

**www.livingrainforest.org/**

### The Microbe Zoo

All you'll ever need to know about micro-organisms such as bacteria. There are some brain-busting words to read along the way.

**http://commtechlab.msu.edu/sites/dlc-me/zoo/**

### The Life Cycle of Plants

A collection of neat little animations which explain topics like seed dispersal really well. There are some worksheets to download as well.

**www.bgfl.org/bgfl/custom/resources_ftp/client_ftp/ks2/science/plants/index.htm**

### Plant Reproduction

Some easy-to-follow animations with text explaining the different stages of plant reproduction. There's a true-or-false quiz at the end too.

**www.ngfl-cymru.org.uk/vtc/20041115/Science/Keystage2/Plants/Plantlife/Introduct/default.htm**

# Materials and Their Properties



## The Challenge of Materials

A zappy page of bits and pieces to help you learn what materials are, why they are used in certain ways and how they are made.

**www.sciencemuseum.org.uk/on-line/CHALLENGE/index.asp**

## Materials Activities

A set of three simple drag-and-drop activities which are a good starting point for learning about materials. Well presented.

**www.crick.northants.sch.uk/Flash%20Studio/cfsscience/Materials1/materialsHtm.html**

## Illustrated Materials Database

A cool way to find out about the different properties of a wide range of materials. It's worth reading the instructions.

**www.activescience-gsk.com/games/index.cfm?module=14**

### Solids and Liquids

This BBC page has an experiment to grow salt crystals, plus some basic information about how materials can change from solids to liquids and back.

**www.bbc.co.uk/schools/podsmission/solidsandliquids/**

### Solids, Liquids and Gases

A set of brilliant little animations which show you what you need to know about these three states of materials. It has a funky soundtrack too.

**www.abpischools.org.uk/resources/solids-liquids-gases/index.asp**

### Digger and the Gang: Separating Mixtures

Help Digger and the gang enjoy their rollercoaster ride by answering the questions about materials in this jolly animation.

**www.bbc.co.uk/schools/digger/7_9entry/8.shtml**

# Physical Properties



## Learning Circuits

This spiffing site will help you to learn all about circuits, mains electricity, switches, components and the rest. There are activities with the information and a glossary.

**www.learningcircuits.co.uk/**

## Electricity Resources

Let Woodlands Junior School guide you to some top places to help you with homework on electricity.

**www.woodlands-junior.kent.sch.uk/revision/Science/electricity.htm**

## Power Up!

Another great site on electricity with facts, background information and activities, all well presented.

**www.electricityineducation.co.uk**

**Forces and Motion: ParkWorld**

This is noisy and wacky but it's a cool way to learn about forces. Click on *ParkWorld Plot* on the home page and follow the instructions

**http://www.engineeringinteract.org/**

**Forces**

Easy to follow, clear and helpful information on a subject which is one of the toughest to understand.

**http://www.zephyrus.co.uk/forces1.html**

**Light: Alien Attack**

Find out which alien is trying to blow up the Earth! A fun way to learn about light – just click on *Alien Attack*.

**www.engineeringinteract.org/interact.htm**

# Physical Properties



## Light Questions

Read the *Fast Facts* on this page then have a go at the questions underneath. Finally look at the answers to see if you were right!

**www.woodlands-junior.kent.sch.uk/revision/Science/light.html**

## Sunshine and Shadow

A very bright and sunny learning activity from the Boots Learning Store which will help you to understand how shadows are formed.

**www.bootslearningstore.com/ks2/shadows.htm**

## Sounds: Ocean Odyssey

Well, the opening story is a bit cheesy but the facts and activities about the science of sound in this animated learning adventure are well worth it.

**www.engineeringinteract.org/interact.htm**

### Sound Questions

Another useful revision page from Woodlands Junior School. Read the facts then try the quiz. Can you get them all right?

**www.woodlands-junior.kent.sch.uk/revision/Science/sound.html**

### Space Explorers

There's a good animation showing how the earth and moon travel round the sun, plus lots more here.

**www.bnsc.gov.uk/learningzone.aspx?nid=3323**

### Earth and Space Links

Here are links to lots of tried-and-tested websites to help you learn about the earth, the moon, the sun and our solar system. Includes games and activities.

**www.woodlands-junior.kent.sch.uk/revision/Science/space.htm**

# Scientific Enquiry



## Natural History Museum

Find out what various 'ologists' do and how they became scientists, plus games, cams and galleries.

**www.nhm.ac.uk/kids-only/index.html**

## The Science Explorer

Lots of experiments for you to try with everyday materials, plus explanations of what is going on.

**www.exploratorium.edu/science_explorer/index.html**

## Reeko's Mad Scientist Lab

Some easy and some tricky experiments for you to try. The science behind the results is explained for you too – phew!

**www.spartechsoftware.com/reeko/**

# History

# General Sites

### History Essentials

Click *History* to start. This site covers Ancient Egypt, Ancient Greece, Romans, Vikings, Tudors, Victorians and World War II. There's not much information but there are useful brief intros, pictures and worksheets.

**www.channel4.com/essentials**

### Walk Through Time

This site's a bit different: it has a good clickable timeline, information about important people and a superb activity called *Odd One Out.*

**www.bbc.co.uk/history/walk/**

### The Learning Curve

A site whose aim is to 'bring history to life'. You'll find documents, film extracts and sound recordings as well as facts about different periods.

**www.learningcurve.gov.uk/**

# Romans

### Romans

Another well-made BBC site, good for homework research. This has facts, a timeline, a glossary, a quiz and printable activities too. Not so many pictures though.

**www.bbc.co.uk/schools/romans/**

### The Romans in Sussex

Bags of good Romans info on this excellent site, plus facts about the Iron Age and Anglo-Saxons. Click *Ages 7-to-11* on the home page first.

**www.romansinsussex.co.uk/**

### Who were the Romans?

You'll find plenty of clear well-illustrated information here for a topic on Romans. Includes a quiz and a great little *What did the Romans do for us?* list.

**www.brims.co.uk/romans/index.html**

# Anglo-Saxons and Vikings



## The Anglo-Saxons

A simple-to-use site with plenty of information, maps, pictures, a glossary, timeline and activities you can print, plus a jolly animated game.

**www.bbc.co.uk/schools/anglosaxons/index.shtml**

## Meet the Vikings

This site from Snaith Primary School has eight questions about the Vikings, each with detailed answers and plenty of illustrations.

**http://home.freeuk.net/elloughton13/vcontent.htm**

## The Vikings

This ace BBC site has sections about Viking life, invasions, beliefs, trade and exploration. You can also find out what happened to the Vikings.

**www.bbc.co.uk/schools/vikings/**

### Tudor Britain

Totally awesome site with amazing graphics such as objects you can open, lots of original sources to see and challenging activities which will get you thinking. Broadband essential!

**www.tudorbritain.org**

### Tudor History

If you're just looking for lots of information and are not bothered about pictures or activities, this is a good place to go. Some of the text is not easy to read though.

**www.tudorhistory.org**

### Tudor Times

A simple-but-helpful primary school site with facts on the main topics you'll need, such as daily life and kings and queens. There's an Elizabethan quiz too.

**www.nettlesworth.durham.sch.uk/time/tudors.html**

# Victorian Britain



## Virtual Victorians

You'll find all sorts on this excellent site, including facts, a great set of pictures of artefacts (with some you can rotate in 3-D), games and a chance to ask a Victorian questions!

**www.victorians.org.uk**

## Headline History

An unusual and interesting site where you get the chance to be a newspaper journalist, reporting on events from history, including Victorian times. There are some great video interviews.

**www.headlinehistory.co.uk**

## Children in Victorian Britain

This splendid BBC site gives plenty of facts in useful chunks along with sound, animated videos, games and worksheets. It covers children at work, play and school.

**www.bbc.co.uk/schools/victorians/**

## The Victorians

An easy-to-navigate site from Nettlesworth Primary School, with plenty of helpful information, pictures and a timeline. It has a good section on important people.

**www.nettlesworth.durham.sch.uk/time/victorian/vindex.htm**

## Victorian Children

A mini-site from Channel 4 Learning which has information, pictures, a timeline and games to help you learn about the life of children in Victorian times.

**www.channel4.com/learning/microsites/Q/qca/victorians/index.html**

## Children's Virtual Museum

Visit a Sainsbury's shop from the end of the nineteenth century and find out what was in it. Some of the content is based on the period just after the Victorians.

**www.j-sainsbury.co.uk/museum/youngvm.htm**

# Britain Since 1930



## World War II

This nifty collection of pages will give you lots of homework help if you're doing a World War II project. Watch out for the useful set of posters.

**www.woodlands-junior.kent.sch.uk/Homework/Britain.html**

## Scotland During World War II

Become a spy to learn about home life, the street, evacuation and school in Scotland from 1939-45.

**www.bbc.co.uk/scotland/education/as/ww2/index.shtml**

## The Home Front

Here are some cool activities plus some great videos of interviews with people who lived through World War II. Broadband needed.

**www.nwlg.org/pages/resources/homefront/**

### Children of World War II

What was rationing like? Was being evacuated scary? What did a wartime home look like? This is a great place to find the answers.

**www.bbc.co.uk/history/ww2children/home.shtml**

### Life in Britain Since the War

This is a bit low on information but there's a useful set of pictures, a quiz and some activities to try.

**http://4learning.co.uk/essentials/history/units/postwar_bi.shtml**

### Britain Since 1948

A simple-but-useful page with sections on technology, fashion, music, travel, home life and more.

**www.grendonunderwood.bucks.sch.uk/our_work/georgina_hewison.htm**

# Ancient Greece

## Ancient Greece

Another brilliant site from the good old BBC. There's lots of information, pictures, interactives, and even extracts from a Greek play to listen to. Wonderful!

**www.bbc.co.uk/schools/ancientgreece/index.shtml**

## Children's Compass

Get a close look at some of the ancient objects from the British Museum's collection. Click *Search* then select *Ancient Greece* and *Find*.

**http://www.thebritishmuseum.ac.uk/childrenscompass/**

## Ancient Greeks

This is a smart place to find lots of facts about life in Ancient Greece. Try the tours and quizzes too.

**www.angliacampus.com/public/pri/history/greeks/index.htm**

# Ancient Egypt

### The British Museum Ancient Egypt Site

A great site, not to be missed if you're working on pyramids, pharaohs, gods, mummies or hieroglyphics. There are cool animations, games and challenges as well as zillions of pictures and facts.

**www.ancientegypt.co.uk**

### The Virtual Egyptian Antiquity Museum

Not the best designed site but it has a fantastic collection of photos, including everything found in Tutankhamun's tomb.

**www.touregypt.net/museum**

### The Mummy Maker

A cool but gruesome game from the BBC. You have to make a mummy using the right tools and methods… or else! A great way to learn about how the Ancient Egyptians preserved the bodies of their kings.

**www.bbc.co.uk/history/ancient/egyptians/mummy_maker_game.shtml**

# Local History



### Your local area in the past

Click *History* then scroll to the right and click on *Your Local Area in the Past.* You'll find activities, ideas, a quiz and pictures, but there isn't much information.

**www.channel4.com/essentials**

### In Living Memory

This page is really helpful if you need some suggestions for starting a local history project. Click the *examples* link to see 14 interviews carried out by other primary school kids.

**www.bbc.co.uk/history/walk/memory_index.shtml**

### Census Investigation

Brilliant set of activities which uses Flash to help you find out about an area of London using real census information from the past.

**www.learningcurve.gov.uk/FocusOn/census/your/intro.htm**

# Geography

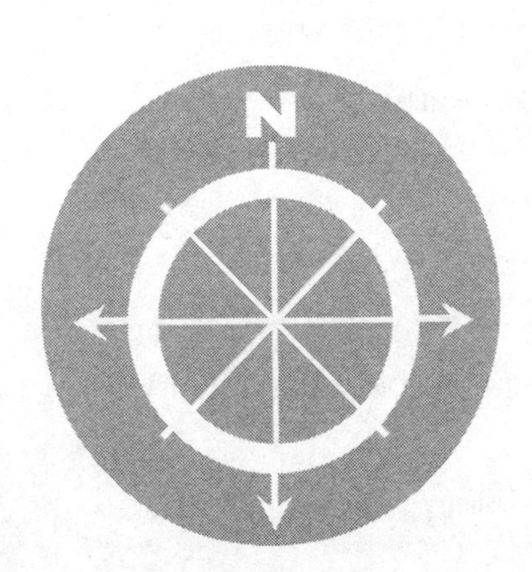

# General Sites



## Geography Essentials

Facts, quizzes, activities, images and more covering a range of topics including people and places, the environment and your local area.

**www.channel4.com/apps26/learning/microsites/E/essentials/geography/index.shtml**

## What is Weather?

This is a simple, fun introduction to the topic of weather. Find out how weather affects people around the world. Recommended.

**www.bbc.co.uk/schools/whatisweather**

## Atlapedia

Tons of facts and figures about the countries of the world.

**www.atlapedia.com/online/country_index.htm**

# Localities in the UK

GEOGRAPHY

### A UK Locality: Flamborough Head

A simple page which contains plenty of information about Flamborough Head in Yorkshire, with photos, map and diagrams you can print.

**www.chester.ac.uk/~mwillard/teacher_education/flapjak.htm**

### Local Traffic

Almost every place in the UK seems to be affected by traffic. Think about this issue in more detail with these pages, which include facts, pictures and a quiz.

**www.channel4.com/apps26/learning/microsites/E/essentials/geography/units/loctraff_bi.shtml**

### Island Life

Discover what it's like to live on two small islands, one off the coast of Northern Ireland and the other off Germany.

**www.bbc.co.uk/northernireland/schools/4_11/tykids/islandlife/index.shtml**

# Localities around the world

## Eye on Brazil

A first-class way to find out about this country and its people. The site is well illustrated, interesting and has lots of nice touches.

**www.globaleye.org.uk/primary_autumn2001/eyeon/index.html**

## India

Here is a simple-to-use guide to this enormous Asian country, with maps, facts, pictures and links to other useful websites.

**www.woodlands-junior.kent.sch.uk/Homework/india.html**

## India for Kids

A fun site with some good interactive features, although the sound on the home page is annoying.

**http://home.freeuk.net/elloughton13/india.htm**

**Mexico for Kids**

There's plenty on this site, although it's a bit slow to load and not always easy to read. But it does tell you how to make a maraca!

**www.elbalero.gob.mx/index_kids.html**

**St Lucia Project**

This is a basic-but-useful site all about the Caribbean island of St Lucia. Find out about its volcanoes and rainforests, and see what happens at carnival time.

**http://www.ict.oxon-lea.gov.uk/st_lucia_project/**

**Africa for Kids**

There's a very good collection of photos on this attractive site plus information about life in four African countries. You can learn how to make great masks too.

**http://pbskids.org/africa/index.html**

# Settlements



## A Virtual Journey

This is a clever site with plenty of helpful resources on settlements. It also features sections on coasts, rivers and pollution.

**www.nwlg.org/pages/resources/geog/hydro_cycle/index.htm**

## Two Cities

Compare Belfast in Northern Ireland with Mexico City in Central America using this clever Flash site from the BBC. Find out what it's like to live in these contrasting places.

**www.bbc.co.uk/schools/twocities/**

## Bangladesh Big Book

This clickable online book is all about Sylhet in Bangladesh. Point your mouse at the bottom right-hand corner of the pages to turn them and see the facts and pictures.

**http://www.bgfl.org/bgfl/custom/resources_ftp/client_ftp/ks2/english/bangladesh_big_book/index.htm**

## A Village Overseas

Click *Geography*, then *People and Places*, then *A Village Overseas*. The information is based on settlements in Malawi in Africa. You'll also find links to other valuable sites.

**www.channel4.com/essentials**

## Living in Brazil

Find out what it's like to live in Brazil. There is a page on street kids and some good general information about the country too.

**www.oxfam.org.uk/coolplanet/kidsweb/world/brazil/index.htm**

# The Environment



## Yowie Environments

A good place to find out about deserts, grasslands, ice caps, woodlands, swamps, rainforests, mountains moorlands and other environments. Find out the threats they face and how they're being protected.

**www.cadburylearningzone.co.uk/env2/index.htm**

## Renewable Energy

There is a lot of very good information here about wind power, solar energy, biomass and other renewables – download the teaching resources for even more.

**www.dti.gov.uk/renewables/schools/index.htm**

## Rainforest Live

This is not the best-designed site but once you've understood the navigation you'll discover plenty of material you can use for a topic on rainforests.

**www.rainforestlive.org.uk**

## Global Warming

Click the *Seven-to-11* link on the home page to discover what global warming is all about. As well as facts, there's a good quiz and some activities to try.

**http://www.defra.gov.uk/environment/climatechange/schools/index.htm**

## Cool Planet

This is the kids page from the Oxfam *Cool Planet* site. Click *World* to find out about 14 countries around the globe and what it's like to live in them.

**www.oxfam.org.uk/coolplanet/kidsweb/index.htm**

## Children's Tropical Rainforests

A well-presented website dedicated to saving the world's rainforests from destruction. There are *Facts* pages which provide good homework help.

**www.magikbirds.com/ctf/index.htm**

# Rivers and Coasts



## River World

This is a splendid resource: a database of rivers with facts, pictures, data, maps and worksheets.

**www.kented.org.uk/ngfl/subjects/geography/rivers/index.html**

## Focus on Rivers

A top-quality place to learn about rivers: it has good graphics and two pages which focus on the Amazon and rivers in Bangladesh.

**www.globaleye.org.uk/primary_autumn2001/focuson/index.html**

## Coastal Environments

Learn all about coasts using this cool interactive big book. It has a glossary, information, pictures, diagrams and experiments to do. The discussion points are excellent.

**www.kented.org.uk/ngfl/subjects/geography/coasts/index.html**

**Mapzone**

A really fantastic interactive site from Ordnance Survey for learning about maps. Click *Homework Help* for map skills and information or try the cool games. Unmissable!

**www.mapzone.co.uk**

**Landscapes**

This a great way to improve your map skills and to learn about the landscapes of Scotland.

**www.bbc.co.uk/scotland/education/sysm/landscapes/**

**Interactive Atlas**

Here's a colourful online atlas you can explore by clicking. There are pop-up boxes of quick facts and you can turn different features on and off. It provides printable maps too.

**www.childrensatlas.com**

# Geography Skills



## Maps of Localities

Need a map to print and colour, or to mark on features? There are lots of different types of maps here – use the links at the bottom for printing.

**www.nationalgeographic.com/xpeditions/atlas/**

## Aerial Photos

This is an amazing site which maps the whole of the UK and provides aerial photos when you zoom in on a particular location. Enter a postcode, type a name or just click!

**http://uk.multimap.com/**

## Freefoto

Thousands of photos which you can use for homework projects. It has a whole section of photos of places in the UK plus others for Europe and the USA.

**www.freefoto.com/index.jsp**

# iCT

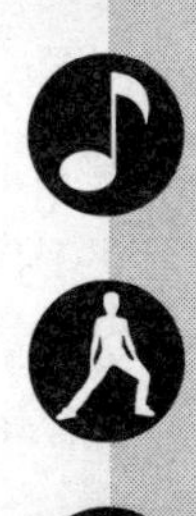

# The internet



## What is the Internet?

A groovy little presentation which uses animations to explain what the internet, worldwide web and email are.

**www.primaryresources.co.uk/ict/flash/email.swf**

## Welcome to the Web

A great site for helping you to discover what the internet is and what it can do. It has useful sections on web browsers, searching and using the internet for research.

**www.teachingideas.co.uk/welcome/**

## Internet Glossary

Do you know what a cookie is? Are you mystified by JPEGs and Java? This online list of web words will help you out.

**http://yahooligans.yahoo.com/docs/info/glossary1.html**

### Think U Know

This site gives advice about using chat rooms safely. It's well designed and fun too.

**www.thinkuknow.co.uk**

### Cyber Café

This is a cool animated activity from Grid Club which teaches you about safety with email, web searching, SMS and chat rooms. Sadly the rest of Grid Club isn't free any more.

**www.gridclub.com/freearea/tasters/cybercafe/base.htm**

### Sid's Online Safety Guide

Let Sid, a rather odd-looking blue boy, teach you how to stay safe when you're using the internet.

**www.bizzikid.co.uk/internetsafety.html**

# Search Sites and Web Tools



## Searching the Net

This excellent presentation explains the skills you need to search the internet successfully. Click the screen to see the slides and move through them.

**http://www.primaryresources.co.uk/online/powerpoint/searching.swf**

## Ask Jeeves for Kids

A safe, simple search engine that you can use to find things on the web. It also has links to useful tools such as an online dictionary, thesaurus and world atlas.

**www.ajkids.com**

## Kidsclick

A collection of links to over 6,000 sites chosen by librarians and arranged into categories. It's useful, but most of the sites chosen are American, once more.

**http://sunsite.berkeley.edu/KidsClick%21/**

## Yahooligans

Another search engine for children. All the sites it finds are checked by teachers and should be suitable for ages seven-to-12, but watch out for the annoying adverts everywhere!

**http://yahooligans.yahoo.com/**

## Web Monkey

Learn how to build a website plus use tools to make slide shows, invitations and work with graphics.

**http://webmonkey.wired.com/webmonkey/kids/**

## Lisa Explains

Good old Lisa! If you're into HTML or web design, or just want to know more about web pages and browsers and how they work, then try this American site.

**www.lissaexplains.com/basics.shtml**

# Using Software



## An Introduction to Spreadsheets

A presentation telling you what spreadsheets are and showing you what they can do. Click the screen to move through the slides.

**www.primaryresources.co.uk/ict/powerpoint/intro_to_spreadsheets_y34.swf**

## What is a Database?

A presentation explaining what databases are and what you can do with them. Click the screen when you've read each slide.

**www.primaryresources.co.uk/ict/powerpoint/What%20is%20a%20database.swf**

## Using PowerPoint

This site is designed for teachers but it is helpful for anyone who wants to learn how to make slideshow presentations using PowerPoint.

**www.actden.com/pp/**

### Graphical Modelling

This is a neat introduction to graphical modelling, which involves using shapes to represent objects in plans or designs.

**http://ngfl.northumberland.gov.uk/ict/qca/ks2/unit5A/graphicalmodelling/index.html**

### Robotics

Use your keyboard to control a robot vehicle just like the ones that NASA sends to Mars. Learn how ICT can be used to operate machines remotely.

**www.thetech.org/robotics/atyourcommand/index.html**

### Quiz Creator

An easy-to-use website where you can make your own multiple choice quiz on any subject. You can save your finished quiz or even email it.

**www2.bgfl.org/bgfl2/quiz_creator/primary/welcome.cfm?l=en**

# Other Sites



## Dance Mat Typing

Learn to touch type with this groovy activity from the BBC – 12 lessons, complete with daft Scouse accent!

**www.bbc.co.uk/schools/typing/**

## Newsround Sci/tech Page

If you want to know about the latest developments in technology, including ICT, then try this superb news page from the BBC – it's interesting, well-designed and constantly updated.

**http://news.bbc.co.uk/cbbcnews/hi/sci_tech/default.stm**

## Free Clipart

Lots of good quality clips from the Northumberland Grid for Learning.

**http://ngfl.northumberland.gov.uk/clipart/default.htm**

# Design & Technology

# General Sites



## Graphic Design

Learn about design drawing, shading, presentation and equipment on this detailed site.

**www.technologystudent.com/designpro/drawdex.htm**

## Equipment and Materials

Learn all about hot glue guns, coping saws, and try squares on this excellent site. It's written for older children but has plenty of useful information.

**www.technologystudent.com/equip1/equipex1.htm**

## Design and Technology Glossary

Know what a mitre block is? Baffled by LEDs and sensors? Go here!

**www.primarydandt.org/learn/glo_0000000318.asp**

**Safety Tips**

This presentation reminds you of the rules you need to follow when doing practical tasks – we don't want any accidents …

**www.primaryresources.co.uk/online/powerpoint/DTsafetytips.swf**

**Science Museum**

London's famous Science Museum has provided this page of links to activities and homework help for all ages. There are several good activities to help with Technology including the *Grain Pit* game and *Flights of Inspiration*.

**www.sciencemuseum.org.uk/education/student/school.asp**

**British Standards Institution**

Activities and games on bridge-building, food packaging and shoes from the British Standards Institution. The *Bridge-Builder* game is a killer!

**www.bsieducation.org/Education/7-11/default.shtml**

# investigating products



**How Stuff Works**

The adverts are a bit annoying but there's loads of detailed information here – find out what's inside a scanner, how text messages are sent and even what's in your breakfast.

**www.howstuffworks.com/index.htm**

**World of Boxes**

This commercial site has some great ideas for designs if you're making boxes. The *pirate treasure chests* are splendiferous.

**www.worldofboxes.com/**

**Hands On Plastics**

Here are facts about plastics plus games and activities to help you learn more about these important everyday materials.

**www.teachingplastics.org/hop_jr/activities/questions/housequestions.html**

## Packaging

Oodles of information here about different forms of packaging and how it works. The navigation is a bit iffy but the site is definitely worth exploring.

**www.dtonline.org/apps/menu/app?2&2&0**

## Bad Designs

Great little site which shows you examples of bad designs from everyday life and makes suggestions for how they could be improved.

**www.baddesigns.com/**

## Vehiclemaster

A simple collection of hundreds of photos of all sorts of vehicles from snowmobiles to limos. Great to give you design ideas for projects.

**www.photovault.com/Link/Vehicles/VEHICLESMASTER.html**

# Food



## Bread

Learn how bread is made in factories then find out about different breads from around the world: tasty stuff!

**www.warburtons.co.uk/curriculum/5b_bread/ideas/2a_pupil.html**

## Hovis

The history of bread, the bread-making process, bread fun facts and info on bread from around the world. Good if you like bread, really!

**www.hovisbakery.co.uk/education/index.html**

## Flour and Grain

Here's a really useful collection of information sheets about flour, grains (including wheat), and bread. Try some of the other links on the page for more information, activities and ideas on food.

**www.flourandgrain.com/homework/7-11.html**

**Yummy Recipes**

Click *Education* then *Cook Club* then *Primary School Recipes* to discover how to make simple kebabs, smoothies and bics. There's also information on kitchen equipment and food skills.

**www.nutrition.org.uk**

**Biscuits**

Click *Items of Work* to see photos of children's biscuits and their designs. This will give you some good ideas if you're working on a biscuits project.

**www.ncaction.org.uk/search/item.htm?id=1358**

**Taste of Success**

Sainsbury's has provided this bank of useful information and pictures about fruit, bread, fish and healthy eating.

**www.j-sainsbury.co.uk/tasteofsuccess**

# Design and Make Projects



## Build a Bridge

Learn all about bridges using this unusual website which has plenty of photos, diagrams and background information.

**www.pbs.org/wgbh/nova/bridge/build.html**

## The Machine Shop

Eight design and technology 'making' projects for you to try. This excellent site has information about tools, plans and extension activities.

**http://ngfl.northumberland.gov.uk/dt/workshop/shopfront.html**

## Mechanical Monkey

Wow! These fabulous wooden mechanical kits will give you some great ideas for things you can make in the classroom.

**www.mechanicalmonkey.co.uk/index.html**

### Finger Puppet Nativity

How cool is this? Dinky little finger puppets you can cut and make from templates. A great way to learn about one of the simplest types of puppet

**www.bbc.co.uk/cbeebies/printables/funmakes/nativity/index.shtml**

### Puppets and Marionettes

Find out how to construct a range of different puppets including stick puppets, bag puppets, finger puppets and marionettes with strings. Follow the illustrated instructions for success.

**www.enchantedlearning.com/crafts/puppets/**

### Protective Equipment

This page has details of a school project on making protective equipment. It's very helpful if you're working on making gloves.

**www.rospa.com/safetyeducation/gloves/diary.htm**

### Mechanical Theatre

This site has some ace videos of mechanical toys called 'automata', which work by turning a handle. See if you can work out how the mechanisms operate.

**http://www.cabaret.co.uk/vrexs.htm**

### Lego Constructopedia

See animated examples of gearing, pulleys, belt drives and other mechanisms which you can make with Technic Lego.

**www.lego.com/education/default.asp?x=x&page=4_1**

### Lever and Linkages

Here are three animated tutorials to explain how you can make simple mechanisms with strips of card and paper fasteners.

**http://ngfl.northumberland.gov.uk/dt/mechanisms/lever%20linkage.html**

# RE

# General Sites



## RE Online

This site has well-organised pages of links for you to find out about Christianity, Judaism, Islam, Hinduism, Sikhism and Buddhism. A lot of the sites listed are not aimed at children, however.

**http://juniors.reonline.org.uk/**

## Religious Festivals

A simple guide to the main festivals of the major religions. It includes facts, photographs and lots of very handy weblinks if you need more.

**www.bbc.co.uk/schools/religion/**

## Woodlands RE Page

This school has produced six good illustrated pages about each of the six major world religions. There are links to other relevant websites and pages too.

**www.woodlands-junior.kent.sch.uk/Homework/Religion.html**

# daism

## ism for Children

y-to-navigate introduction to the Jewish
he site design is a bit iffy but there's
of helpful information and some
raphs, with links to other sites.

**chool.eduweb.co.uk/carolrb/judaism/judai1.html**

## Jewish Connection

usual but well-designed site which
s on four Jewish people from Stoke
nt. There are answers to basic
ns about their faith and links to
nformation.

**t-staffs.co.uk/synagogue/index1.htm**

## gogues

er ace site from a primary school,
a virtual tour of a synagogue. Good
s, clear information and glossary links
d.

**ams.suffolk.sch.uk/synagogue/index.htm**

# Christianity

## Educhurch

Fantastic visual website which features three different UK churches. There are tours of the buildings, pics galore, videos, and information, plus some fab interactive features.

**www.educhurch.org.uk**

## RE: Quest

Wow! There is an incredible amount of good stuff on this site all about Christianity. Check out the songs, video clips and amazing virtual tours of churches.

**www.request.org.uk**

## RE Thesaurus

I'm not sure that 'thesaurus' is the right word but, anyway, click on *Christianity* and you'll find a list of topics with links to helpful sites which explain them.

**http://juniors.reonline.org.uk/juniors_thesaurus.php**

# Christianity



## Creation

This striking animation puts pictures to the first few verses of the Book of Genesis from the Bible, describing God's creation. Recommended.

**www.k4t.com/eng_creation.htm**

## The Nativity Story

Here's a very simple presentation of the story of the first Christmas. It's a simple slide show with words and pictures – well presented, and useful if you've forgotten the story!

**www.topmarks.co.uk/christianity/nativity/index.htm**

## Christmas Pages

The graphics are grim, the music drives you batty, but there is a lot of information here about Christmas traditions and Christmas customs around the world. Turn the sound off!

**http://atschool.eduweb.co.uk/carolrb/christmas/christmas1.html**



## The Easter Story

A simple, easy-to-read
the Easter story in slid
pictures.

**www.topmarks.co.uk/christiani**

## Happy Easter

Facts, activities, cards t
and information about
all in all, a very jolly sit

**www.happy-easter.com**

## Harvest Festival

A basic-but-helpful pa
celebrate Harvest Fes
harvest traditions and

**www.woodlands-junior.kent.sc**

# Ju



## Juc

An ea
faith.
plenty
photo

**http://a**

## Th

An ur
centre
on Tre
questi
more

**www.spi**

## Syn

Anoth
offerin
pictur
includ

**www.hit**

### Hanukkah

A breezy introduction to the Jewish festival of lights, Hanukkah. Plenty of info, along with pictures and audio files of songs. There's a good glossary too.

**www.ort.org/ort/edu/festivals/hanukkah/index.html**

### Torah Scrolls

Find out about the sacred writings of the Jewish faith on this nifty junior school page. There are links to other pages on Judaism.

**www.hitchams.suffolk.sch.uk/synagogue/torahscrolls.htm**

### The Story of Moses

Moses is a key figure in the Jewish religion and his story is a real cracker. This slide show is easy to follow and well presented.

**www.topmarks.co.uk/judaism/moses/index.htm**

# Hinduism



## Hinduism for Schools

Click the Key Stage 1 buttons rather than the Key Stage 2 and 3 ones, as the content is much easier to understand.

**www.btinternet.com/~vivekananda/schools1.htm**

## Introduction to Hinduism

A very basic page of information and pictures which explains what the faith is and about its founders, holy writings and prayers.

**www.hinduism.fsnet.co.uk/schools1p1.htm**

## Hindu Beliefs

Hindukids is a flashy site which takes quite a long time to load, so you'll need broadband. There is a glossary and lots of learning resources to try out.

**www.hindukids.org/learn**

## Hindu Temple Tour

High quality and high tech, this site offers a video tour of a Hindu temple, interactive pictures, information and stories. Click *Subjects* then *RE KS2* then *Gujurat Hindu Temple*.

**www.cleo.net.uk**

## Holi

Find out about the Hindu festival of colours, Holi, with this cool slide show. Click each slide when you have read it.

**www.primaryresources.co.uk/re/powerpoint/Holi.swf**

## Diwali

Find out all about the Hindu festival of lights, Diwali. This is a good primary school site with stories, facts, illustrations and useful links.

**http://home.freeuk.com/elloughton13/dday.htm**

# islam



## Islam 4 Schools

Find out about Allah, being a Muslim, prayer, prophets, children in Islam, and plenty more with a simple question-and-answer approach.

**www.islam4schools.com/infant.htm**

## BBC Newsround Special: Islam

Excellent guide to Islam, featuring lots of clear explanations of the faith plus pictures, videos, news reports and more.

**http://news.bbc.co.uk/cbbcnews/hi/specials/2005/islam/**

## The Qur'an

Here's a basic page of information about the holy book of the Muslim faith.

**http://atschool.eduweb.co.uk/carolrb/islam/holybook.html**

## Islamic Festivals

A page of links to sites which will tell you all about Ramadan, Eid and the Hajj.

**http://juniors.reonline.org.uk/topiclist.php?84**

## Mosques

This is perfect if you need to find out about mosques. There is a virtual tour with plenty of photos, clear information and an explanation of words. Great work by Sir Robert Hitcham's School.

**www.hitchams.suffolk.sch.uk/mosque/default.htm**

## The Hajj

Impressive site about the big annual Muslim pilgrimage to Mecca. Take the animated *Virtual Hajj*, read about its history, see videos and more.

**www.channel4.com/life/microsites/H/hajj/**

# Sikhism



## Sikhism

Good basic introduction to the faith with plenty of facts but not many pictures.

**www.bbc.co.uk/schools/religion/sikhism/**

## The Five Ks

Simple slideshow to introduce the five 'Ks' which Sikh people wear. Click the screen to move each slide on.

**www.primaryresources.co.uk/online/powerpoint/Sikhism.swf**

## Sikhism for Children

The is a helpful website if you need a simple introduction to the Sikh faith. It has a glossary, illustrations and links, but the presentation is – well, judge for yourself …

**http://atschool.eduweb.co.uk/carolrb/sikhism/sikhism1.html**

## Watford Sikh Gurdwara

Virtual tour of a Sikh place of worship. Lots of good photos but not much information here.

**www.thegrid.org.uk/learning/re/pupil/sikh/**

## The Story of Rajni

Cool interactive story about the Sikh Golden Temple. Click *Subjects* then *RE KS2* then *The Story of Rajni*.

**www.cleo.net.uk**

## Sikh Festivals

A dull-but-info-rich page about the various Sikh festivals and ceremonies held at different times. Don't expect graphics!

**www.sikhs.org/fest.htm**

# Buddhism



## Buddhism

Basic primary school website about the Buddhist faith. Look for the buttons at the bottom of the page for more info.

**http://website.lineone.net/~jlancs/buddhism.htm**

## The Story of the Buddha

Simple online slide show with line drawings and text. You can download it or print it too.

**www.buddhanet.net/e-learning/buddhism/storybuddha.htm**

## Stories from Buddha's Life

A well-presented set of online stories which help explain who Buddha is. There are fun online activities too (these open in pop-up windows).

**www.dharmaforkids.com/Buddha/story/story.htm**

**Buddhist Robes**

Why do followers of Buddha wear robes and what do they symbolise? Roll your mouse over the picture to find out.

**www.dharmaforkids.com/Sangha/robes/robes.htm**

**Buddhist Worship**

This page has links to sites which have photos and information about Buddhist places of worship and pilgrimage.

**http://juniors.reonline.org.uk/topiclist.php?32**

**Festivals**

This page from the BBC is about Wesak, or Buddha Day. There are questions and answers plus lots of facts, but it's a bit thin on visuals, sadly.

**http://www.bbc.co.uk/schools/religion/buddhism/buddha_day.shtml**

# Other useful sites for RE



**Newsround Guides**

Here you'll find links to all sorts of useful mini-guides to topics such as religious festivals, asylum seekers, the Middle East, patron saints and the Archbishop of Canterbury.

**http://news.bbc.co.uk/cbbcnews/hi/guides/default.stm**

**RE XS**

This site has a section called *Interact* which has questions and answers for pupils, connected with RE. Look through the archive to see what is there.

**http://re-xs.ucsm.ac.uk/**

# Art

# investigating art



## Primary Art

A cracking site about how to create murals. There are some great videos which show different painting techniques, plus slide shows of children working, and a gallery. Give it a butcher's.

**www.bbc.co.uk/northernireland/schools/4_11/primaryart**

## Landscape Adventure

Learn about how artists create landscape paintings in this great interactive site, then have a go at creating your own landscape picture online.

**www.sanford-artedventures.com/play/landscape1/index.html**

## The Artist's Toolkit

Find out how artists use colour and line, shape, balance and space. There are animations, activities and videos as well as information. Splendid.

**www.artsconnected.org/toolkit/**

## CBBC Art

Loads of cool stuff here: online workshops, art ideas, facts about artists, galleries and activities.

**www.bbc.co.uk/cbbc/art/**

## Art Detective

This is a really clever idea: solve the mystery of Grandpa's painting by following the clues and answering questions. A natty way to learn about pictures.

**www.eduweb.com/pintura/index.html**

## Kidzone

You'll love this all-action site from Artisancam. There are videos, activities, interviews with artists, online activities, workshops, information and galleries of work.

**www.artisancam.com/kidzone**

# Artists

## Canaletto

Find out how this great artist used perspective to make his painting more realistic: a really good interactive animated slide show. Click *Canaletto*.

**www.artisancam.com/kidzone**

## Inside Art

A very cool way to learn about meister Dutch impressionist Van Gogh – you're sucked into a painting and have to escape!

**www.eduweb.com/insideart/index.html**

## Van Gogh Workshop

Online lesson about Vincent Van Gogh, plus painting activity. Click *Key Stage* 2 then *Art* then *Painting* then *Landscape Van Gogh Style* then the activity link.

**www.ngfl-cymru.org.uk/vtc-home.htm**

**Artisancam**

This is a great way to learn about the work of various living artists – there are videos of artists at work, showing how they carry out different techniques, plus much more. Not to be missed.

**www.artisancam.com**

**Art Adventures**

If you need basic information about a range of artists, styles and art media, then here is a very useful page of links.

**www.sanford-artedventures.com/study/study.html**

**Leonardo's Workshop**

Find out about the work of this great painter with this fun online adventure activity. There's a lot to read but it's good stuff.

**www.sanford-artedventures.com/play/leonardo/index.html**

# Galleries



## The National Gallery

Find images of great paintings organised in different ways, learn about artists, and try out some activities in the *Art Action Zone*.

**www.nationalgallery.org.uk**

## Tate

Here is online access to a collection of British art from 1500 onwards and international modern art. Collections of paintings, drawings, photos, sculptures, ceramics and much more can be searched in different ways.

**www.tate.org.uk**

## Washington DC National Gallery of Art

This is the kids' site of the gallery and it has a great collection of things to do, plus a guide to searching the museum's huge collection of pictures and objects from all over the world.

**www.nga.gov/kids/kids.htm**

# Drawing and Painting

### How to Use Watercolours

This has an excellent step-by-step guide, plus sections on materials and the history of watercolours.

**www.bbc.co.uk/cbbc/art/howto/watercolour**

### Looney Tunes: Learn to Draw

Impress your friends with your ability to produce a brilliant Bugs Bunny or a rockin' Road Runner with this awesome cartoon site.

**http://looneytunes.warnerbros.co.uk/looney_library/learntodraw/library_draw.html**

### Access Art: Drawing

Click *Drawing Together* for worksheets and more on backgrounds, storyboards, characters and animations.

**www.accessart.org.uk/workshops_drawing.php**

# Drawing and Painting



## Artyfactory

Learn about pencil shading, Egyptian art, African masks and perspective with these detailed online workshops.

**www.artyfactory.com**

## Create Art

Do you want to know how to draw faces? Or blend coloured crayons? Or use watercolour pencils properly?

**www.sanford-artedventures.com/create/create.html**

## Impressionism

If you want to learn about this famous art movement then there is a great slide-show introduction here. Click *Experience Impressionism*.

**www.impressionism.org**

# Other Arts and Crafts

**Smart Makes**

Find out how to make collages, prints, 3-D work and all sorts of funky pieces of artwork with the BBC's Smart.

**www.bbc.co.uk/cbbc/art/smart/makes/index.shtml**

**Sculpture Workshops**

Online workshops for ages seven upwards from Access Art. These will help you learn what sculpture is and give you ideas for making your own sculptures from everyday objects.

**www.accessart.org.uk/workshops_sculpture.php**

**Art Attack**

A stonking collection of step-by-step guides to creating all sorts of work, especially 3-D pieces, using everyday materials. Loads of photos, tips and inspiration.

**www.hitentertainment.com/artattack/**

# Other Arts and Crafts

## Weave

Cool slide show with animations which show how to weave a basket out of card. There are other workshops on drawing and collage too. Click *Weave*.

**www.artisancam.com/kidzone**

## Finger Tips

Wow! If you're looking for ideas for art – especially 3-D – there are tons here. Good photos and instructions too.

**www.foundationtv.co.uk/f-tips**

## The @rt Room

Ideas, inspiration, information about all sorts of art.

**www.arts.ufl.edu/art/rt_room/index.html**

# Digital Media

## Digital Palette

This site is all about how computers can be used to generate art. You can see work done by other schools and there is an image bank of brilliant photos for you to use.

**www.content.networcs.net/digipal/flash/digipal_intro.swf**

## Painting Trees

Use a computer painting programme to create a vivid picture of trees.

**www.hitchams.suffolk.sch.uk/ict_art/trees/progression.htm**

## Artpad

This is so cool! Paint a picture using the simple tools, then watch a replay of how you made it. Save it and send it to someone by email.

**http://artpad.art.com/artpad/painter/**

# Clipart

## DK Clipart

Fabulous collection of top-notch pics and photos from Dorling Kindersley. Illustrate your homework with a touch of class.

**http://uk.dk.com/static/cs/uk/11/clipart/home.html**

## Discovery School Clipart

Lots of clips organised in subject categories. Click the one you want, then right-click it to copy it so you can paste it into a document.

**http://school.discovery.com/clipart/**

# MUSIC

# General Sites



### Music Glossary

Do you know what 'forte' means? Ever get your tempo mixed up with your timbre? You're not the only one! Click on *Glossary of Terms* to see a mini-dictionary of musical words.

**www.nwlg.org/pages/resources/pmusic/index1.htm**

### The Music Room

Great place to learn about orchestras, instruments, composers and much more. There are audio files to hear music plus games to play, and it's well designed.

**www.dsokids.com/2001/rooms/musicroom.asp**

### BBC Children's Music

The BBC has lots of great resources for music including facts, pictures, audio files, activities and games where you can compose your own pieces.

**www.bbc.co.uk/music/childrens/**

### Music Encyclopaedia

Here you'll find information about music, instruments and composers with good illustrations. It's not easy to read but it does cover a lot of ground.

**http://library.thinkquest.org/10400/html/**

### Composers

If you need information about the lives of the great composers such as Mozart, Bach or Vivaldi, this page has links to sites with information.

**www.cdli.ca/CITE/composer.htm**

### Virtual Orchestra

A simple-but-excellent site where you can see photos of instruments and hear them being played. There's not much information though.

**http://ngfl.northumberland.gov.uk/music/orchestra/contents.htm**

# investigating music



## NYP Kidzone

An awesome site from the New York Philharmonic Orchestra. It has a composers' gallery with information, an instrument section where you can hear music, games, instrument-making workshops and lots more. Unmissable.

**http://www.nyphilkids.org/main.phtml**

## Music by Arrangement

You can download free sheet music for recorders and other instruments from this site. The pages are in PDF format so you'll need the free Adobe Acrobat Reader.

**www.musicbyarrangement.co.uk/schoolband/**

## Play Music

If you need to find out facts about the instruments used by an orchestra, and would also like to hear them, then this site is the business.

**www.playmusic.org/stage.html**

### Musical Mysteries

You'll enjoy this gamey site from the BBC – it has some good animated activities to help you learn about rhythm and mood, amongst other things.

**www.bbc.co.uk/northernireland/schools/4_11/music/mm/index.shtml**

### The Street

There are five musical families from five different countries on this street. Click the instruments to find out about them or listen to some music and read about local musicians and their styles.

**www.bbc.co.uk/radio3/world/onyourstreet/thestreet/**

### Drum Kits and Rhythms

Cool site with loads of information about drums and rhythm, plus pictures, videos, sounds and links to games and activities.

**www.hitchams.suffolk.sch.uk/ictmusic/drums/index.htm**

# Composing



## Music Games

Here is a set of cool games from the BBC which allow you to make music. Try the *Beatmachine* for percussion or the fabulous *Composer* to create your own piece to email.

**www.bbc.co.uk/music/childrens/games/index.shtml**

## Creating Music

This is a good place to try some composing using a range of simple-to-use online activities. You might need to install some special Quicktime software for it to work (instructions are given).

**www.creatingmusic.com/**

## Make a Guitar

Instructions here for how to make some simple DIY instruments including a guitar, a rain stick and a peg shaker.

**www.bbc.co.uk/cbbc/music/make**

# Understanding Music

## Music Theory

Wow – this great site has free online lessons which teach you all about the theory of music from the most basic areas to much more advanced levels. There are interactive tests too.

**http://www.musictheory.net/**

## Introduction to Reading Music

This site takes you through the basics step-by-step and has a neat feature where you can listen to the music shown in each part.

**http://datadragon.com/education/reading**

## Music Sense

Groovy little interactive guide to what's what in music. Hear notes, play with pitch, mess about with chords and scales.

**www.bbc.co.uk/music/parents/activities/musicsense/index.shtml**

### Music Education Centre

This site has a section called *What is Music?* which includes a guide to different types and styles of music plus a lot of other detailed background information.

**www.geocities.com/npasupathi**

### Happynote

This site has free software to download which teaches you about listening and music theory. Make sure you ask before you download this software!

**www.happynote.com/music/learn.html**

# PE

# General Sites



## CBBC Sport

This funky page links to games, interviews with sports players and a handy section of facts about over 100 different sports.

**www.bbc.co.uk/cbbc/sport/index.shtml**

## BBC Sports Academy

This is a great site if you're already playing a sport and want to sharpen up your skills. There are videos with tips by top players and athletes, sections on rules and equipment, and much more.

**http://news.bbc.co.uk/sport1/hi/academy/default.stm**

## Our Kids Sports

This is a basic portal site with useful links for the sports listed. The links appear on the right-hand side when you have clicked a sport on the left.

**www.ourkidsports.com**

**Newsround Sport**

Up-to-date sports news, stories, information, guides and links to other useful areas such as health and fitness.

**http://news.bbc.co.uk/cbbcnews/hi/sport/default.stm**

**Links4kids**

Hundreds of links to hundreds of sites about loads of sports, from aerobics to the Winter Olympics.

**www.links4kids.co.uk/sports.htm**

# Health and Fitness



## Galaxy H

Gen up on health and fitness here. Find out why you need to exercise and if you're getting enough of it. Plenty of well-presented info and some games and activities too.

**www.galaxy-h.gov.uk/**

## Kids' Health

Advice from the BBC about looking after your body. Includes an animated tour of the body and notes about healthy eating, exercise and drugs.

**www.bbc.co.uk/health/kids/**

## Boots Learning Store

This site has information about health for ages seven-to-11. It covers topics such as skin care, sunshine, eyesight, hygiene and breathing.

**http://bootslearningstore.com/home.htm**

**BAM!**

Flashy site which covers physical activity, healthy eating, diseases, safety and body information. Try the *Motion Commotion* test to see what sports could be right for you. (Warning: it's very American!)

**http://www.bam.gov/**

**Kidnetic**

Fantastic American site all about health and active living. Try out the amazing *Move Mixer* dance game where you have to design a dance then join in.

**www.kidnetic.com/**

**Games Kids Play**

Simple site devoted to playground games and skipping rhymes plus games for PE. Low on graphics but well worth a look.

**www.gameskidsplay.net**

### Youth Dance England

There's not a lot on this site but it does have a useful map with links to local organisations running dance activities near you.

**www.yde.org.uk**

### Dance Links

If you want to know about different forms of dance from around the world, this site has links to lots of useful websites. They're not aimed at children so some may be hard to read.

**www.sapphireswan.com/dance**

### The Spring Board

A website for junior gymnasts. There's not much information here but it tells you where you can find out more. There is a gallery and messageboard.

**www.british-gymnastics.org/springboard/**

## Gymnastics Glossary

This is where you can find out what a pike position is and learn about handsprings. A simple dictionary but it has some video links.

**www.usa-gymnastics.org/gymnastics/glossary.html**

## Swimming

Look down the page for links to animations showing you the strokes, tips from top swimmers, facts and links to other useful sites. Excellent.

**http://news.bbc.co.uk/sport1/hi/other_sports/swimming/default.stm**

## Safe Swimming

This site has information for parents and teachers as well as children, with a few activities which you can print out.

**www.nc.uk.net/safeswimming/index.htm**

### Netball Links

Love netball? This page has links to sites about the game including rules, equipment, facts, leagues, organisations, coaching hints and more.

**http://www.ucl.ac.uk/~uczcw11/baseres.htm**

### Junior Football

Become the next Rooney! Find out where you can play locally, read or send in match reports, and learn more about the beautiful game …

**www.bbc.co.uk/juniorfootball/**

### FA Games Room

A good place for fun footy games online. Try volleying or bending free kicks like Beckham.

**www.thefa.com/Features/Postings/2005/04/TheGamesRoom**

## Youth Athletics

If you want to know more about running, jumping and throwing events on track and field, then try this site. It will help you find out about clubs and events in your area and has links to information sites.

**www.boja.org/**

## Rugby Guide

Find out about scrums, lineouts, flankers, rucks and mauls. Lots of information about rules, plus a rugby dictionary.

**www.scrum.com/rugby_guide/default.asp**

## Raw Tennis

This is the website of a tennis skills programme from the Lawn Tennis Association. You need to register to get full value from it.

**www.rawtennis.net**

# Other Sports



## Kidsrunning

If you're into running then you'll find plenty to interest you on this US site. The design's a bit yucky, but you can't have everything …

**www.kidsrunning.com**

## Hockey Online

Click on *Young People* for the children's pages on this official hockey site. You'll find info about how to play and where to find local courses so you can learn more.

**www.hockeyonline.co.uk**

## BBC Olympics

Want to find out about Olympic sports such as archery, badminton, cycling, fencing, rowing, sailing, volleyball and many more? Look here!

**http://news.bbc.co.uk/sport1/hi/other_sports/4306126.stm**

# PSHE & Citizenship

# General Sites

## Citizenship Foundation

Click the *Young People* tab at the top of the home page to get to information, things to do and downloads about subjects such as money, law and politics.

**www.citizenshipfoundation.org.uk**

## Planet.com

Find out what you can do to stop the environment from being damaged. Info and activities about water, energy, recycling, cars, rich and poor, food and bio-diversity.

**www.channel4.com/learning/microsites/P/planet/menu.html**

## Galaxy H

There's plenty to do on this site while you learn about: relationships, good health, staying safe, drugs, and taking risks. Click *Voyagers* to start.

**http://www.galaxy-h.gov.uk**

### Citizen Power

This will get you thinking: facts, opinions and activities all about topics such as power, rights, animal welfare, voting, war and crime.

**www.channel4.com/learning/microsites/C/citizenpower/index2.htm**

### Global Gang

Killer site all about the developing world. Click *Homework Help* to find out about hunger and fair trade, or to learn about disasters and refugees. Games and quizzes too. Nice.

**www.globalgang.org.uk**

### Newsround

It's good to keep informed about what's going on in the world. This is the website of the BBC's Newsround TV news programme. It's constantly updated, and it's interesting and well designed.

**http://news.bbc.co.uk/cbbcnews/default.stm**

# Making Choices



## Yheart

Learn how exercise, drugs and diet can affect your heart and your health. Make the right choices with this site.

**www.bhf.org.uk/yheart**

## Dare Kids

Games and stories about the dangers of drugs. If you want information click *Dareteens* on the left of the home page.

**www.darekids.co.uk/**

## Cycle Smart

Disney have put together this funky site with tips on looking after your bike and riding safely. Plenty of sound, action and good advice.

**www.disney.co.uk/DisneyChannel/cyclesmart/main.html**

## Fire safety

This is a subject that needs to be taken seriously. This excellent site for ages seven-to-eight will give you the facts and help you to act wisely in an emergency. It has some neat little Flash games too.

**www.firekills.gov.uk/juniors/index.htm**

## Get Firewise

If you're nine-to-11 and need to learn about fire safety try this superb interactive site: clear information, quizzes, activities and fun games will help you learn.

**www.firekills.gov.uk/seniors/index.htm**

## Healthy Kids

Tons of information here and all well presented: pages on decision-making, drugs, feelings, weight, spots, growth and much more.

**www.healthykids.org.uk**

# Making Choices



## It's Up To You

Another good site from the BBC – this one is about healthy eating choices. There are good animations and lots of helpful facts.

**www.bbc.co.uk/northernireland/schools/4_11/uptoyou**

## Inside Outside

Six Flash games about making good health choices involving: teeth, strangers, litter, exercise and bullying.

**www.ltscotland.org.uk/healthykids/demo/**

## Cyber Café

Great online game about safety with email, web searching, SMS and chat rooms from Grid Club. Well worth a try.

**www.gridclub.com/freearea/tasters/cybercafe/base.htm**

# Other useful sites



### Childline

Click *Kid Zone* to see what this site can offer to children who need help. There's a problem page with questions and answers, plus details of where you get help with all sorts of things.

**www.childline.org.uk**

### Hedgehogs Road Safety

Luckily you can turn off the slightly annoying music on this otherwise good site all about road safety. There are some good games and plenty of advice and information.

**www.hedgehogs.gov.uk**

### Playground Fun

Get exercise and stay fit by playing games in the playground at school. This site has lots of suggestions from old favourites to, well, new favourites.

**www.playgroundfun.org.uk**

# Other Useful Sites



## Media Smart

A site all about TV and advertising. There's a clever little Flash game where you can make your own TV advert.

**www.mediasmart.org.uk/kids/index.html**

## Boots Learning Store

Click *Pupil*, then *Seven-to-11*, then choose the activity about health issues such as skin, head lice, sun care, eyesight, healthy lungs and clean hands. Lots of good noisy Flash activities here.

**www.bootslearningstore.com/home.htm**

## Britkid

This is a really interesting site all about racism. It looks at what it's like to live in Britain today through the eyes of children of different cultures.

**www.britkid.org**

**Bullying Online**

Full of advice from victims of bullying and other people, suggestions for avoiding bullying, and information about what to do if you are being bullied. You can email the site for help too.

**www.bullying.co.uk**

**Kidscape**

More helpful advice about bullying. There's a very good page of ways to protect yourself.

**www.kidscape.org.uk/childrenteens/childrenteensindex.shtml**

**NSPCC**

A site with the aim of preventing child abuse. Good advice about bullying, internet safety and what to do if you need help.

**www.nspcc.org.uk/homepage2**

# General Reference

**For internet search sites see page 78, in the ICT section**

# Encyclopedias

## Encyclopedia.com

Free online encyclopedia. You can find information either by browsing or typing in a search query. It has a dictionary and thesaurus too.

**www.encyclopedia.com**

## Fact Monster

A good starting point if you need quick facts and information about places, people, events and so on. It includes a search engine and a homework page, but it is American so watch out for 'math' and 'soccer'!

**www.factmonster.com**

## Britannica

Another big online encyclopedia. This has short free articles on each subject but you have to join to get more detail and pictures. The search results may be tough to read too.

**www.britannica.com**

# Atlases



### Children's Atlas

This clickable atlas has some neat features such as wildlife symbols you can click and facts about countries, but the maps are not very detailed.

**www.childrensatlas.com**

### Encarta Atlas

Just click to zoom in and get more detail, or use the arrows. The maps are good but you'll need broadband otherwise it's so slow you'll fall asleep.

**http://encarta.msn.com/encnet/features/mapcenter/map.aspx**

### Streetmap

Type in the name of a place in the UK or a postcode, then click the results to see a map of the place. There are buttons to zoom in and out to get large- or small-scale maps too. Nice.

**www.streetmap.co.uk**

# Dictionaries and Thesauruses



### Online Dictionary

This online dictionary is aimed at children, so is simpler than most others on the web. Just type in the word you want to look up.

**www.wordcentral.com**

### Wordsmyth

Another internet dictionary for children. Make sure you type your word in the children's dictionary search box.

**www.wordsmyth.net**

### Thesaurus.com

This online thesaurus is not a children's version but it's quite easy to use. Just type in a word to bring up lots of synonyms – make your writing more interesting!

**www.thesaurus.com**

### Woodlands Junior School

Here's a really useful page from this outstanding school website. Lots of links to websites, games, activities, reference sites, and more. Homeworktastic!

**www.woodlands-junior.kent.sch.uk/Homework**

### Topmarks

The creators of this marvellous site deserve top marks, by gum! You can search for websites by menu or key word, or use the *Subject* and *Age Group* drop-down menus.

**www.topmarks.co.uk**

### SOS Teacher

Here are hundreds of answers to hundreds of homework questions from kids. The answers are written by teachers – make sure you click the right age group first.

**www.bbc.co.uk/schools/sosteacher/index.shtml**

# General Homework Sites

## Homework Help

A long page of links to different sites, organised by topics. The sites are recommended by librarians so you can blame them if you don't like them!

**www.iwight.com/library/children/homework.asp**

## Ambleweb

You're bound to find something useful on Ambleside Primary School's stupendous and vast website. Use the drop-down menus at the top to choose a subject.

**www.amblesideprimary.com/ambleweb/numeracy.htm**

## Homework Elephant

Has plenty of sites listed, but watch out because some of the links are broken and a few of the sites are not right for the seven-to-11 age group suggested. The *Hints and Tips About Homework* section is particularly useful.

**www.homeworkelephant.co.uk/index.shtml**

# Revision Sites

See individual subjects for more revision sites.

# General Revision Sites



**BBC ReviseWise**

This is a well-organised, helpful and fun-to-do set of resources from the BBC. It only covers English, maths and science but there are games, activities, factsheets and worksheets too.

**www.bbc.co.uk/schools/revisewise**

**Channel 4 Learning**

Choose your subject and look for websites that say KS2. Some are brilliant, some wacky, some cool and some a disappointment, but you're sure to learn plenty.

**www.channel4.com/learning/teachers/websites**

**Woodlands Revision Corner**

Start clicking here and you'll discover a mega collection of games, activities, information and useful sites to help you revise for Y6 SATs. Well worth adding to your favourites.

**www.woodlands-junior.kent.sch.uk/revision/index.html**

# Top 10 Homework Tips

# TOP 10 HOMEWORK TIPS



### 1. Do homework sooner rather than later

If you put it off you might end up too tired or you might run out of time and make a pig's ear of it.

### 2. Find a quiet place

Get away from the TV, escape your noisy little sister or brother, and find a corner of peace and calm. Ahh!

### 3. Make sure you know exactly what you need to do

Read the question or task, then read it again. Go on. There's nothing worse than handing in five pages about smileys when you were supposed to write about similes.

### 4. If you don't understand the task, ask!

A parent, adult you know, or even older brother or sister might make the question clear in a couple of ticks, thus saving you hours of brain-ache.